Pass It On

Ultimate Reflections on Life and Death

By Laynee Gilbert
and Ann

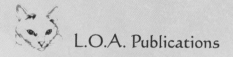
L.O.A. Publications

Cover and interior photos © 2005 by Marcie Gilbert.
Design and layout by Marcie Gilbert and Patricia Krebs.

First edition published 2005 by L.O.A. Publications.

L.O.A. Publications
P.O. Box 6107
San Jose, California 95150-6107
LOApubs@aol.com
www.loapublications.com

ISBN-10: 0-9678966-1-4
ISBN-13: 978-0-9678966-1-8

Other books by Laynee Gilbert:
The Complete Dream Journal
I Remember You: A Grief Journal

Pass It On

Ultimate Reflections on Life and Death

By

_____

Once you learn how to die, you learn how to live.
Morrie Schwartz, from Tuesdays with Morrie
by Mitch Albom

It was my uncle's 75th birthday. A few days prior he had received an ominous diagnosis: his leukemia had returned. Since he had already undergone extensive chemotherapy the year before, the prognosis wasn't good. What gift could I give to this person to whom material goods mean less than nothing? *You can't take it with you... what's important is what you leave behind.*

Then it dawned on me – what better gift than a book to write his stories and lessons in, to leave behind a piece of himself. The search was on.

There were no books available that fit the bill. There were empty journals, but this was a man who had never done journal-writing before, and I was concerned that the book would remain empty without something to help draw him out. I finally bought him a collection of quotes and a blank book, with a note that said, "One to inspire thoughts, the other to record them."

The seed for this book was planted.

A few years passed, and the seed lay dormant. Then suddenly the seed sprouted, when I learned that my dear friend Ann was diagnosed with a very aggressive cancer that would take her life in just a few short months.

Ann was an inspiration to me in both her living and her dying. She was utterly honest and open in how she faced her life as well as her death. Over the years we'd spent many hours in conversation about everything from politics to personal experience, and I deeply respected her deliberate views and passionate opinions. She had a keen crap-detector, with no patience for pretense. For various reasons best left unsaid, life for Ann was very painful. So in an odd yet understandable way, she almost welcomed her final prognosis.

One day she shared with me a quote she'd read that spoke to her about the death experience she was embarking upon, and that was the moment when the seed broke through the ground and into sunlight. I told her about my idea for *Pass It On*, and together we made it a reality. She gathered quotes and provided personal insights that helped shape my words, and I bound our efforts together within these pages.

Ann lives on, not just in my memory, but in this book that is now in your hands. This is what she and I have passed on to you.

Now fill the book with your essence, and pass it on.

I'm not really afraid to die, but I find it hard to imagine
the world continuing on without me in it.
Ann

Getting Started

If journal-writing has been a natural part of your life, then you
probably require little guidance to get started with this book.
However, one thing that sets this experience apart from other
journal-writing is that typically a journal is written primarily for the
privacy of oneself, while the contents of this book are intended for
sharing. If the idea of disclosing your innermost personal
reflections with another feels somewhat scary or intimidating to
you, imagine what an honor it would be if someone special were to
share their deepest thoughts and feelings with you before they
parted. Consider this: *There is nothing left to hide.*

For some, writing in the form of a letter to someone else can help
facilitate the flow. What important ideas have you formulated over
the years, or in the past few hours? What lessons did it take a
lifetime to learn that you want to impart to another? If you're not
sure where to start, the images and quotes within these pages are
designed to help elicit thoughts and feelings about this season of
your life. Start with one that particularly speaks to you, and then
allow the words to pour out uncensored.

Other Ways to Pass It On

If writing does not appeal to you or feels too laborious for you right now, there are other ways you can use this book. Ann had never been too interested in journal-writing herself, so she imagined that the book could sit on her coffee table, and when family and friends came to visit, they could write a favorite memory of times spent together. In the days that followed, she could enjoy reading through the pages, and then later when the book was passed on to her children and grandchildren, they could learn more about her through the stories of others.

These pages can also enfold personal notes and cards that friends have sent, serving as a central holding place for meaningful memorabilia that's been sitting in a drawer or hidden away on a shelf. As you pull these pieces together, imagine your loved ones later perusing through them, weaving together an intricate tapestry of a life they knew some about, but in fact had so much more to discover.

In Closing

When someone close to us dies, we grieve the loss of that person. When we're the one dying, we grieve the loss of everyone and everything we've ever known.

What I've learned from walking with Ann, with my uncle, and with my mother before them, is that each of us writes a unique and complex verse in the eternal song, and each of us walks through this final passage in our own inimitable way.

As you fill the pages of this book, relish in the opportunity to present others you care about with a more complete view of all that you are and have been. With your gift comes the possibility to continue shaping the world through the custodians who live on with your legacy, until their destiny inevitably meets your own.

Before you pass away, pass it on.

Few of us live beyond our three score and ten years and yet in that brief time most of us create and live a unique biography and weave ourselves into the fabric of human history.

Elisabeth Kübler-Ross

I'm explicitly making my life a teaching, by expressing the lessons that I've learned through it, so it can become a map for other people. Everybody's life could be like that, if they choose to make it so; choose to reflect what they've been through and to share it with others.

Ram Dass

Birth is a beginning
And death a destination.
And life is a journey,
A sacred pilgrimage –
To life everlasting.

Jewish Prayer

When we finally know we are dying,
and all other sentient beings are dying with us,
we start to have a burning, almost heartbreaking sense
of the fragility and preciousness of each moment and each being,
and from this can grow a deep, clear, limitless compassion for all beings.

Sogyal Rinpoche

Death? Why this fuss about death. Use your imagination, try to visualize a world without death!
...Death is the essential condition of life, not an evil.

Charlotte Perkins Gilman

To let go of the last moment and open to the next
is to die consciously moment to moment.

Stephen Levine

The idea of death, the fear of it,
haunts the human animal like nothing else;
is a mainspring of human activity – designed largely to avoid the fatality of death,
to overcome it by denying in some way that it is the final destiny of man.

Ernest Becker

Wisdom begins at the end.
Daniel Webster

I am a greedy, selfish bastard.
I want the fact that I existed to mean something.
Harry Chapin

To every thing there is a season, and a time to every purpose under heaven.

Ecclesiastes 3:1

Religion is the human response to being alive and having to die.

F. Forrester Church

If my doctor told me I had only six minutes to live,
I wouldn't brood. I'd type a little faster.
Isaac Asimov

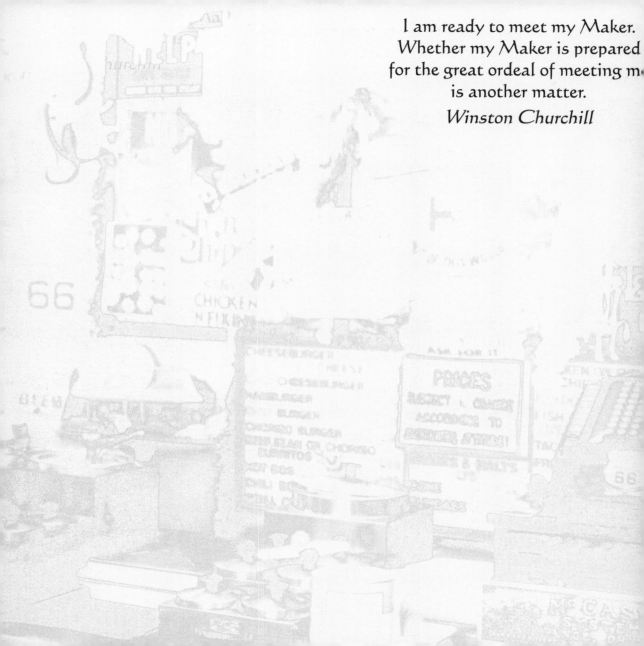

I am ready to meet my Maker.
Whether my Maker is prepared
for the great ordeal of meeting m
is another matter.
Winston Churchill

And, when he shall die,
Take him and cut him out in little stars,
And he will make the face of Heaven so fine
That all the world will be in love with night
And pay no worship to the garish sun.

William Shakespeare

It is foolish to be afraid of death.
Just think.
No more repaired tires on the body vehicle,
no more patchwork living.

Paramhansa Yogananda

Life is pleasant.
Death is peaceful.
It's the transition that's troublesome.

Isaac Asimov

Fear not death,
  for the sooner we die,
    the longer we shall be immortal.
                    Benjamin Franklin

Death and taxes and childbirth!
There's never any convenient time for any of them.
Margaret Mitchell

After your death you will be what you were before your birth.
Arthur Schopenhauer

The stroke of death is as a lover's pinch,
Which hurts and is desired.
William Shakespeare

Disease generally begins that equality which death completes.
Samuel Johnson

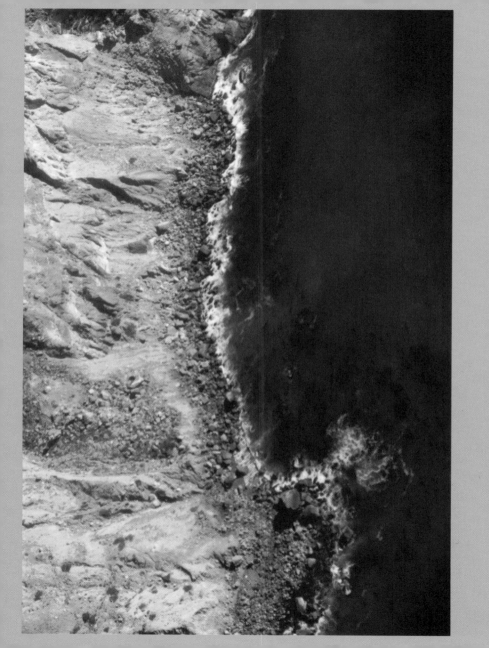

Death is the wish of some, the relief of many, and the end of all.

Lucius Annaeus Seneca

That which is so universal as death must be a benefit.
Friedrich Schiller

Death is beautiful when seen to be a law and not an accident –
It is as common as life.

Henry David Thoreau, 11 March 1842,
letter to Ralph Waldo Emerson

Out, out, brief candle!
Life's but a walking shadow,
a poor player that struts and frets his hour upon the stage
and then is heard no more.
It is a tale told by an idiot, full of sound and fury, signifying nothing.
William Shakespeare

No one can confidently say that he will still be living tomorrow.

Euripides

On a large enough time line, the survival rate for everyone will drop to zero.
Chuck Palahniuk

Here's my suggestion to the skeptics and "experts," for a refreshing change of pace.
We're done proving that there's life after death.
We've proven it well past our own satisfaction.
From now on, let's do it this way: You prove that there's not.

Sylvia Browne

I'm not afraid to die, I just don't want to be there when it happens.
Woody Allen

Way out

This platform for
Lochailort
Beasdale
Arisaig
Morar
Mallaig

I wanted a perfect ending.
Now I've learned, the hard way, that some poems don't rhyme,
and some stories don't have a clear beginning, middle, and end.
Life is about not knowing, having to change,
taking the moment and making the best of it,
without knowing what's going to happen next.
Delicious Ambiguity.
Gilda Radner

Death is no more than passing from one room into another.
But there's a difference for me, you know.
Because in that other room, I shall be able to see.

Helen Keller

Life is the art of drawing without an eraser.
John W. Gardner

Here is the test to find whether your mission on Earth is finished:
if you're alive, it isn't.

Richard Bach

Do not dwell in the past, do not dream of the future,
concentrate the mind on the present moment.
Buddha

Why does a person even get up in the morning?
You have breakfast, you floss your teeth so you'll have healthy gums in your old age,
and then you get in your car and drive down I-10 and die.
Life is so stupid I can't stand it.

Barbara Kingsolver

Maybe all one can do is hope to end up with the right regrets.
Arthur Miller

When we remember we are all mad,
the mysteries disappear and life stands explained.
Mark Twain

Life would be much easier if I had the source code.
Unknown

Nature does nothing uselessly.

Aristotle

Time is but the stream I go a-fishing in.
Henry David Thoreau

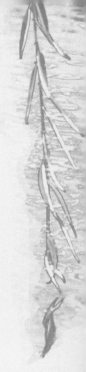

The more sand that has escaped from the hourglass of our life,
the clearer we should see through it.

Jean Paul

The
only
true
wisdom
is
in
knowing
you
know
nothing.

Socrates

It is as natural to die as to be born;
and to a little infant perhaps the one is as painful as the other.
Francis Bacon

We sometimes congratulate ourselves
at the moment of waking from a troubled dream:
it may be so the moment after death.
Nathaniel Hawthorne

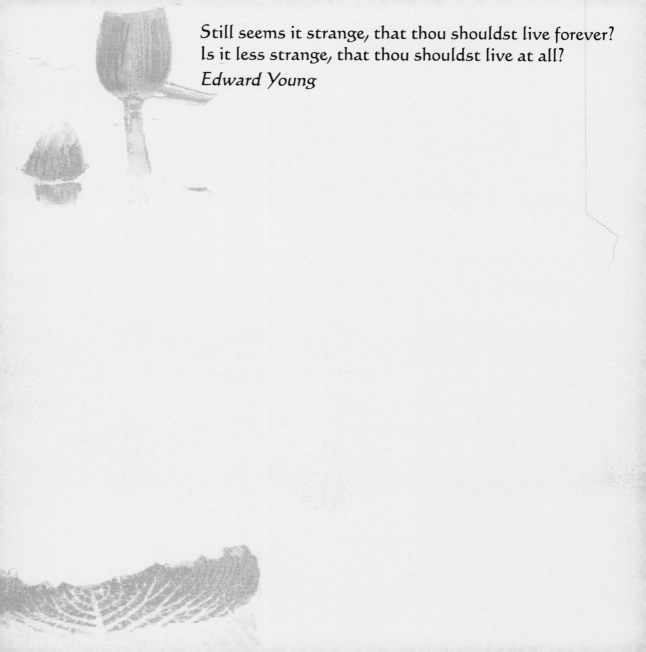

Still seems it strange, that thou shouldst live forever?
Is it less strange, that thou shouldst live at all?

Edward Young

Our lives are waves that come up out of the ocean of eternity,
break upon the beach of earth, and lapse back to the ocean of eternity.
Some are sunlit, some run in storm and rain;
one is a quiet ripple, another is a thunderous breaker;
and once in many centuries comes a great tidal wave that sweeps over a continent;
but all go back to the sea and lie equally level there.

Austin O'Malley

I asked the leaf whether it was frightened
because it was autumn and the other leaves were falling.
The leaf told me,
"No. During the whole spring and summer
I was completely alive.
I worked hard to help nourish the tree,
and now much of me is in the tree.
I am not limited by this form.
I am also the whole tree, and when I go back to the soil,
I will continue to nourish the tree.
So I don't worry at all.
As I leave this branch and float to the ground,
I will wave to the tree and tell her,
'I will see you again very soon.'"

That day there was a wind blowing and, after a while,
I saw the leaf leave the branch
and float down to the soil, dancing joyfully,
because as it floated it saw itself already there in the tree.
It was so happy.
I bowed my head,
knowing that I have a lot to learn from that leaf.

Thich Nhat Hanh, Peace Is Every Step:
The Path of Mindfulness in Everyday Life
(Bantam Books)

About the Author
Laynee Gilbert, M.A., is a counselor and writer.
Other books to her credit include *I Remember You: A Grief Journal* and
The Complete Dream Journal.

About the Photographer
Marcie Gilbert is a freelance photographer, teacher,
and the author of the children's picture book, *Zee... Adventure One: Borrowing China.*
She is also Laynee's sister.

About Ann
I've lived my three score and ten, and now I'm glad to be immortalized in this way.
It's a great privilege to be leaving behind something that will continue on in the world,
even without me in it."